Strong, Bold, and Courageous

Thanks!
meadow
faith

Strong, Bold, and Courageous
Words of Wisdom from a Fifth Grader
From A to Z

By Meadow Faith Wharton
with Jennifer Wharton

Strong, Bold, and Courageous
Words of Wisdom from a Fifth Grader From A to Z
Copyright © 2019 by Meadow Faith Wharton

ISBN 9781691273003 (paperback)

For more information,
Name: Meadow Faith Wharton
Website: www.meadowfaith.com
Instagram: itsmeadowfaith

Cover design: Arunodoyart
Content contributors: Jennifer Wharton, Jared Wharton

This paperback edition first published in 2019

Printed in the United States of America

DEDICATION

\ \ \ \ \ \ \ \ \ \

To my family,
Thank you for being there for me, loving me
unconditionally, teaching me, supporting me, and
always being my biggest cheerleader.
I love you all so much!

To my friends,
Thank you for your encouragement
and for having my back!

CONTENT

\ \ \ \ \ \ \ \ \ \

INTRODUCTION

\ \ \ \ \ \ \ \ \ \

I love to read. Ever since I was little, I wanted to grow up and have my very own library. But how awesome would it be to write a book? Now I'm just a kid, what could I possibly write about or have to say?

As you will get a glimpse in the pages to follow, last year I learned some tough life lessons on friendships, the ugliness of gossip, the effects of bullying, the HUGE problem of kids coming to school hungry and the disruptive behavior by classmates that made it hard for a teacher to teach and students to learn.

One night while my mom and I were reading a book together and talking about some of the things going on at school, my mom used the book as an example and said "Meadow you could write a book like this but make it your own. It could be a book about words of wisdom you could impart to your peers". My eyes lit up, my mom said, and I became so excited. That very night we decided to use the alphabet as a guide, and I chose the words that came to my mind immediately for each letter.

In our home, no matter what kind of student you are, we have to do summer school work and have a reading list. However, this summer, instead of doing workbooks, my mom said I could start writing. So that's exactly what I did, and this book is what was created.

So to answer my question, "what could I possibly write about or have to say?" Well, it turns out I had a lot to say.

We are all works in progress. Although I make mistakes all the time, I try my best every day to learn, grow, and apply these life principles within this book. I hope that you would read a letter each day and think of ways you can apply whatever speaks to you to your life.

Learn, apply, grow, and flourish.
That is my goal every day!

ATTITUDE

Definition: Your opinions and feelings about someone or something that affect how you behave.

A healthy attitude is essential. Your attitude isn't just what you say, but also reflected in how a person chooses to carry themselves. Your attitude tells a person what you act like, what your personality is like, and if you would be a good friend. Many different influences surround us. Some are not the best. Having a positive attitude is a choice you have to make. Just like how you present yourself to the world is a choice.

What kind of attitude do you want to reflect?

Imagine if your P.E. teacher told you to find a partner. Would you choose a partner that is the kid who is never paying attention, gets in trouble all the time, has terrible grades, and is rude to everyone? No way, I know you're thinking to yourself, I would pick a good kid! You want to choose the kid that is a good sport, team player, encouraging and will help you do a good job.

No one wants to be around a person that has a negative attitude.

Last school year, someone took a present that was given to me by my friend, out of the gift bag that was hanging from my desk. He and another student proceeded to play keep away with it without my permission. I had a choice to make and decided to calmly take a deep breath and tell him to please give it back to me. He ignored me, and I repeated myself three times, and he finally decided to listen and gave it back to me. I was agitated from the situation, and at any time, I could have gotten angry, but I chose not to get a bad attitude, and keep calm.

Here are a few things that I practice that help me when I feel frustrated, stay in control, and choose to have an uplifting attitude.

1.   Don't react right away. Take a deep breath.
2.   Ask God to help you.
3.   Ask yourself how you can positively handle the situation.

Now, remember that we all need to work on our attitudes.

B RAVE

Definition: Someone who is unafraid to face danger, difficulty, or pain.

Being brave doesn't mean you have to go on an adventure and fight some mythical creature like a dragon. There are many different ways we can be brave every day. Have you ever stuck up for a friend when someone was rude to them? That was brave. Have you ever raised your hand in class when the teacher asked a question, and nobody else did? That is brave. Have you ever told the truth about something you did even though you knew you would get in trouble? That is brave.

Being brave starts on the inside. Sometimes being brave means you have to face your fears. Just like the example above where you are sitting in class, and the teacher asks a question, and nobody raises their hand. You feel like you know the answer, but the thought enters your mind, "what if I'm wrong, and everyone laughs at me?" Should you give in to that fear and not participate at all? No, think about this. If no one else in the class raised their hand, then they probably didn't know the answer either, or they were just scared. By you attempting to answer the question, you jump into action by facing your fear and move forward into bravery.

Now, I want to talk about another B word that is a massive problem throughout our schools in our country. Statistics show one out of every five kids has reported being bullied,* but what about the kids who don't say anything? We know that the number is much higher.

Forms of Bullying:

Verbal Bullying:
Cruel words to harass and threaten.

Physical Bullying:
Hitting, kicking, pinching, spitting, pushing, shoving, tripping, etc.

Social Bullying:
Spreading gossip and lies.

Cyber Bullying:
Online bullying

As you can see, there are many ways of bullying. I have encountered kids being rude, saying nasty things to me, taking my things, harassing me at recess, throwing rocks and balls at me and gossiping. It was tough, and made me feel incredibly lonely. Not only did I not understand why these things were happening to me, I felt frustrated because no one should have to experience these types of behavior from their peers.

Let's talk about being brave when you see someone who is being bullied or mistreated. No one likes to be called a "tattletale" or "snitch," but likewise no one likes being called cruel names and harassed, so you have to make the decision to be brave and get help. I had to make this decision myself. All I wanted was for the behavior to stop. I wanted to go to school and feel safe. I wanted to go to school and learn. I wanted to go to school and experience peace. I don't have control over how other kids behave, but I do have control over how I respond. When I told a trusted adult what was happening, the situation was resolved immediately, and the next day when I came to school, the behavior stopped towards me.

So, how do we handle bullies? We speak up! If we stay silent, we are adding to the problem instead of using our voice to be a part of the solution and putting a stop to the bullying behavior.

If you see someone being bullied or mistreated in any way, I urge you to be brave and help. Help by telling an adult, help by talking to the kid who is being mistreated, help by sticking up for them. It is never okay for anyone to mistreat you.

Here are a few ways you can use your voice and be brave!

1. Stand up for yourself and anyone you see being bullied.

2. Speak firmly, and while saying their name, ask, "Why would you say that?" or "Stop it!"

3. Tell a trusted adult. (Parents, teachers, yard duty, principle, bus driver.)

4. Support classmates that are bullied.

5.   Share kindness; it's contagious. *More on this in the next chapter.

6.   Show compassion.

7.   Be respectful.

When other kids see you standing up against bullying, other kids will start to stand up as well!

Bullying in America

Bullying is unwanted, repeated, aggressive behavior that uses an imbalance of power to intimidate or humiliate others. Did you know that about 20% (1 in 5) kids between 12 and 18 are bullied every year? 160,000 teens skip school every day to avoid bullying. This leads to 1 in 10 kids who eventually drop out of school entirely due to bullying. Sadly one in four teachers see nothing wrong with bullying, and according to dosomething.org, will only intervene 4% of the time they witness bullying.

So be BRAVE, and DO SOMETHING!

https://www.dosomething.org/us/campaigns/step-bullying/community

CONTAGIOUS

Definition: (of an emotion, feeling, or attitude) likely to spread to and affect others.

When you think about the word contagious, you automatically think of sickness. Sickness can be contagious; one person gets sick, then that sickness soon gets passed onto another person then that person spreads on that sickness to another person, and so on. This cycle creates a chain reaction. But other things are contagious too, like a negative spirit and likewise a positive spirit.

Now when I say the word spirit, I'm not talking about someone who occasionally is in a foul mood or temporarily upset about a situation. We are human and have emotions, but what I'm referring to is a person's character as a whole.

Definition of Spirit - qualities regarded as forming the definitive or typical elements in the character of a person, nation, or group or in the thoughts and attitudes.

When your spirit is negative, it affects everyone around you.

Have you ever been in a room full of people and someone walked in, and the whole atmosphere of the room changed? You felt their presence. That is how strong our spirit is! Another example is when you make a new friend; sometimes you start acting like them, saying the same things they say or liking the same things they are interested in. It's okay if these are good things, but this is why it is vital to choose your friends wisely. You don't want to end up with a friend who is always negative, gossiping about others, mean spirited, disrespectful and rude or you're in trouble!

Think of a negative spirit as a sickness, and a positive spirit as healing for that sickness. A friend in a bad mood all the time will only bring your good mood down, make you feel down and cause you pain. But a good friend will always find a way to bring your spirit back up, tell you you can do it and is kind. Good and bad attitudes are like enemies on opposite sides.

My mom always says, "If someone is being more of an influence on you in a negative way than you are on them in a positive way; its time to move on."

Here are a few ways that I make sure I have a positive, healthy spirit.

1.   Start each day with positive thoughts/prayer.

2.   Choose three words to confess out loud each morning. For example, I am Strong, Bold, and Courageous.

3.   Show compassion. If someone needs help, help them!

4.   Choose to forgive before someone does you wrong.

5.   Smile. We all can use a smile.

6.   Walk-in love. When love is in your heart, you attract goodness.

D IVERSITY

Definition: Each individual is unique. These can be along the dimensions of race, ethnicity, gender, sexual orientation, socio-economic status, age, physical abilities, religious beliefs, political beliefs, or other ideologies.

Diversity is beautiful, and we should all embrace it.

We are all different, unique individuals that have a purpose on this planet. Some of us are brown, white, tan, dark, light, tall, short, small, big, have curly hair, straight hair, red hair, blonde hair, brown hair or black hair. Some of us have blue eyes, green eyes, brown eyes, or hazel eyes. We are from all sorts of different cultures, countries, states, and backgrounds. Some know one language, and others know several. We are all different, and our differences should be celebrated.

I was blessed to grow up in a home that celebrates diversity. I am full white, but my two older siblings are of mixed race, half white and half black. When I was little, I saw no difference in us at all because I knew nothing more than they were my big brother and sister. Now that I am older, I see all of our differences, but they don't matter.

We are all different shades, sizes, and textures of God's beauty.

For the first four years of my life, I lived in Bamberg, Germany, where I heard the beautiful German language and was exposed to their amazing culture and food. Back here in our home state of Washington, we go to a huge church that I am proud to say represents over 100 nationalities. Once a year we have International Sunday, and everyone comes dressed in their traditional outfits and holding their birth country flag. It is quite a beautiful thing to see.

It is essential to our family to walk in love and embrace all differences, and I am thankful.

At school, church, sports, and your neighborhood, I would challenge you to befriend kids who don't look like you. Instead of staring, smile! Ask questions if you have them and be open to making a new friend. If someone dresses differently than you, respectfully ask him or her about their traditional clothing. If someone is disabled, instead of avoiding them, you can ask them kindly if they care to share with you their story.

I remember meeting a Medal of Honor war hero at my Dad's business. He had a mechanical hand that was pretty cool but also somewhat creepy looking. He stuck out his hand to shake mine, and at first, I was hesitant because it wasn't a "normal-looking hand," but when he saw that I was a little scared he started telling me about what happened and I realized that I didn't need to be afraid. His story was of him being brave, and although he lost his hand, technology has made it possible for him to have a mechanical hand which allows him to be able to do everyday functions that he wouldn't be able to do without it, like shake my hand, and I think that is pretty amazing.

Excited

Be excited!

Be excited about life; you don't want to live a miserable life, so enjoy it and be passionate about what the future could bring you! Make life fun and surprising. Be open to try new things, situations, foods, and places. Our family loves to explore new things. We hike, go on bike rides, travel, try new restaurants, other cultures, and love to have a great time every day no matter how big or how small the activity.

Staying excited about life can be hard sometimes. For example, when you make a mistake, get in trouble, or you don't get your way. It can be hard to snap out of your foul mood. My mom always tells me, "Meadow, just because one thing didn't go your way doesn't mean it has to ruin your whole day." For me, this is very hard because I will pout about something until I can work it out in my own way. But, I'm learning in life; not everything is a choice or negotiation. There is always a reason why things are a certain way or why I can't do something when I want to or how I want to.

If we get our minds off of ourselves and onto everyone around us such as classmates, family and or friends, then we can think of what is better for everyone involved and not just yourself.

Be excited to experience life with all the people that are in your world and cross your path.

"It is not happy people, who are thankful,
It is thankful people who are HAPPY."
- Author Unknown

\ \ \ \ \ \ \ \ \ \

F ORGIVE

Definition: To stop being angry with someone, or to stop blaming the person for doing something.

A lot of things can be hard, but in life, releasing forgiveness seems to be one of the hardest things to do. Having a forgiving spirit is very important because if you don't forgive, you will be holding on to grudges and that will only cause you pain.

Unfortunately, I recently had an experience with this. It was brought to my attention that a friend told a mutual friend; all these horrible lies about me. I was so hurt. Every time I would see her or think of her, I would get angry all over again. I just didn't get it. Why makeup things that are not true and then spread that gossip around? The more I thought about it, the angrier I would get so I had to accept that I would never understand why. I then chose to pray and release forgiveness. And eventually, all my pain went away.

Forgiveness means you release compassion towards a person you feel wronged by even when you still don't have answers or understand why.

Here is a word on forgiveness that my mom wrote that I want to share:

TRUE forgiveness starts with confessing it (saying it out loud). It doesn't mean you even want to at the time, but it's a start. By you saying it every day, or every time that person comes to mind. God will begin to heal that hurt. Releasing forgiveness is an ACTION, not an emotion or feeling. It's a choice. Even in your anger, pain, and or misunderstanding, choose to let go and move on. Our feelings and emotions will remind us of the constant pain the person did to you. It will put you on the roller coaster ride of torment only IF you let it.

On the other side of forgiveness is reconciliation. If you don't desire to reconcile, then you don't truly forgive! This is a very hard fact to accept. Some have had horrible things done to them by another person. Full forgiveness might be a process that takes years of healing, depending on the seriousness of the situation. The important thing though is to start. Reconciliation doesn't mean that you trust that person again. Trust is to be rebuilt over time and may never fully be achieved at all.

In some cases, it might mean you never allow that person the opportunity to hurt you again. But you forgive them, have no ill thoughts towards them, there is peace between you and you chose to love them from afar.

If you release forgiveness and seek to reconcile, but the other person doesn't do the necessary steps towards that reconciliation; you've done your part and continue to walk in it. Un-forgiveness harbors anger, bitterness, and hatred in your heart, further giving the other person power over you, and that is the last thing you want to do.

Guess what! People are going to hurt and offend you. People say stupid things and do silly things. Sometimes un-intentionally and sometimes intentionally. And here is the kicker SO DO YOU! I know I say things all the time that I wished I didn't say, or it sounded better in my head, and when I spoke it out loud, I instantly regretted it. No one is perfect. Including YOU!

Each morning when you wake up, know that at some point in your day, someone will more than likely offend you or hurt your feelings. So before they even do, forgive them! If you choose to forgive before the offense has even been committed I promise the sting will not be as sharp.

Here are a few ways to walk a life in forgiveness.

1. Say out loud every day; I forgive "person." Even if you don't want to, I challenge you to start saying it every time that person comes to your mind. I promise over time; it will get easier.

2. Pray about it. Prayer has a way of mending our broken hearts.

3. If you are able, talk to them about how you feel. Most of the time, things are not always what they seem. A little communication goes a very long way.

4. Choose to be <u>understanding</u> even when you <u>don't understand</u>. Agree to disagree.

Giving

Definition: Freely devote, set aside, or sacrifice for a purpose.

Have you ever heard the saying "It is better to give than to receive"? When you give a person you care about a gift, doesn't it make you feel good inside? I know I feel so good when I can give my friends or family members a gift. I get so excited!

Giving can be done in many ways. You could give your time, money, and food, to name a few. Some situations happen all around us every day that we can look for ways of being more giving.

For example:
- Your classmate needs a pencil,
- Your teacher needs a helper,
- Your classmate is struggling with a math problem,

- Your parent needs help bringing in the groceries, with dinner, or cleaning up the house

You get the point. There are so many opportunities all around us that you can give and be helpful.

Do you ever go to lunch and see a person without lunch to eat? This is something that I have seen way too often, and it bothers me so much! No child or person should ever go hungry, especially at school. This is a huge problem.*

Every person's home situation is different. Some families struggle and don't have money for things your family might. We should never make someone feel bad because they don't have lunch. We don't need to know "why" we need to try and help if we can. Do you ever have extra lunch money in your pocket or any additional food in your lunch? Giving doesn't mean you have to give money; it could be as simple as bringing extra food in your lunch to someone who doesn't have a lunch. Maybe you can ask your parents to provide you with a little extra in your lunch in case you see a child that doesn't have lunch?

My church motto is Live to give, Love to give. Isn't that an excellent life motto to live by? I sure think so!

Childhood Hunger in America

Childhood hunger in America is a serious issue. About 1 in 5 children are lacking proper, nutritious food. At my school, this means 4 FULL classrooms could have kids who aren't getting enough to eat daily.

16.2 million children live in households that lack the means to get enough nutritious food regularly.

20% of food-insecure families are not eligible for government assistance. Meaning they earn too much money to qualify for the programs but still can't afford to put healthy food on the tables at home.

But I'm just a kid, what can I do? Your Mayor, Governor, State Representative, and Senator: they work for you! Call them! Write them! Get your Mom, Dad, Brother, Cousin, friends and teachers, and anyone you know to tell them that we need to strengthen and improve the programs that feed kids and create ways to access programs like free summer meals and school breakfast.

https://www.feedingamerica.org/take-action/advocate

https://www.nokidhungry.org/what-we-do/child-hunger-advocacy

Hopeful

Definition – Believing that what you wish for will happen.

The word hopeful reminds me of one of my favorite Scriptures Hebrews 11:1
"Now **faith** is confidence in what we **hope** for and assurance about what **we do not see**."

This scripture is merely saying that we use our faith for things we are hopeful for but do not have yet or can physically see. In other words, you have confidence (faith) that your parents are going to give you a Christmas gift that you ask for, but it's not Christmas yet, and you don't have it or see it. Ha! I'm hopeful that makes sense.

We live in a world that is full of bad things happening all the time. From the news reports local and far, social media sites and word of mouth, we are always hearing and seeing things that are not good.

From cell phones, laptops, iPads, Facebook, Instagram, Snapchat, T.V., books (all the things), Technology has been so good in so many areas, but it has also changed our world dramatically. We not only see and hear about what is local to us but everything all over the world and in a matter of seconds. If we aren't careful about what we are consuming, we can quickly become negative, scared, complaining individuals.

So how do we protect ourselves and stay hopeful? How do we also not become numb and insensitive to the extremely "real life" horrible things that happen when we see/hear about them all the time? How do we empathize, show compassion and love when we are so overexposed to tragedy it becomes normal? How do you remain optimistic in a cynical world?

These are all great questions and one we talk about in our home often. In short, I will list a few ways our family stays focused, full of love, and hopeful.

1. Don't watch the news. If it's that important, trust me, you will hear about it.

2. Don't watch shows or read things that are not good for your soul.

3. "Unfollow" anyone who is negative, complains or shares anything that causes division. The great thing about the "unfollow button is that you are still friends, but you don't see all the garbage, and they don't know you're not reading it!

4. Focus on the good. There is so much good going on all around us.

5. Surround yourself with optimistic "happy" people/friendships.

6. Learn how to shut down conversations that are talking bad about another person no matter who they are, and if you know them or not. That includes celebrities and politicians. Gossip is just nasty!

7. Choose to walk in love, compassion, grace, understanding, and forgiveness every single day!

Our world isn't perfect, but when we focus on the positive and all the good, it's easier to be hopeful!

I MAGE

Definition:
1. An idea of how something looks.
2. A representation of something.
3. The way a person appears to other people.

How do you see yourself? Do you think positive thoughts about yourself? Do you see yourself as a kind, compassionate, loving person? Do you love yourself? I'm not talking in an arrogant or bragging sort of way but in the way of confidence and security.

Self-esteem isn't self-absorption; it's self-respect.

Did you know that you are a "one of a kind" MASTERPIECE? Do you believe that? I sure hope so. No matter what you look like, YOU are a powerful human being created to do amazing things on this earth!

We are all unique in our own ways. Our bodies, race, hair, eye color are some of our physical differences. Some bodies have disabilities, are tall, short, curvy, or slim. Our hair is all different; some have short, long, fine, coarse, curly, kinky, straight, wavy, frizzy, brown, red, black, blond, auburn, golden the list goes on and on. So many spectacular differences!

Just as we are different by physical appearance, we are also different from so many other aspects as well from culture, environment, traditions, religions, styles, personalities, temperaments, interests, talents and so on. We are truly one of a kind, and our differences should be celebrated, uplifted, complimented, and embraced.

All this talk about hair reminds me of one of my big sisters. Two of my siblings are half black and white. My sister has naturally beautiful brown curly hair. For years she straightened it because she wanted to have straight hair like our mom. Even though my whole family would tell her how gorgeous her hair was, at the time, she didn't embrace it. As she matured into a young woman, she has embraced her curls and rocks them. Occasionally she straightens her hair, but she has learned to celebrate what she was given, and that is one of the things I admire about my big sister.

So how can we improve how we see ourselves? I believe it takes time and tons of practice. Developing good self-esteem involves encouraging a positive attitude toward yourself, the world around you and appreciating your worth.

Here are a few suggestions you can put into practice that can help you form a more positive self-image of yourself.

- Don't be mean to yourself.
If you have a negative thought, tell yourself, "stop it" and think of something that you like about yourself!

- Focus your thoughts.
Instead of focusing on what you think are your negative qualities, focus your attention on your strengths.

- You are perfectly IMPERFECT.
NO ONE is perfect – Strive to do YOUR best. Allow yourself to make mistakes. Try laughing instead of criticizing.

"No matter how educated, talented, rich or cool you believe you are,
how you treat people ultimately tells all."
- Unknown Author

\ \ \ \ \ \ \ \ \ \

J UDGING

Have you ever heard the expression "don't judge a book by its cover?" Well, this applies to people as well. We should never judge a person based on their looks, race, disability, beliefs, religion, or style.

We all have different things that we are into, but it doesn't mean that yours is better than another's. It's just different. Maybe a kid likes rock music, but you do not. Does it mean that you have nothing in common with that person at all? Perhaps not, but what if you had something in common and you never gave that person a chance all because you judged them based on them liking rock music? You might not ever discover that that same kid loves the show Stranger Things as much as you do and you would enjoy sharing your thoughts about the latest episode or season with them.

What if you are really into the latest style trends, but a kid in your class doesn't care about fashion statements? Does it mean that you don't have anything in common at all? Does it mean that you make fun of that person for having a different style than you do?

These examples might seem like stupid reasons to not be friends with someone, and you would be right. Although, we see and hear of these types of judgments all the time and way more serious ones.

You get the point though. We should never judge a person based on such superficial reasons. There is so much more to people than their outward appearances. Get to know a person before deciding if you want to be friends. You might be surprised that you have more in common than you first thought.

KNOW IT ALL

Definition: A know-it-all is a person who constantly presents their input as though they were professionally trained, schooled or have firsthand insight into subjects when it is evident this is not the case.

Have you ever been around a person who thinks they know it all? Someone who has an opinion about everything? It could be any subject, and they believe annoyingly they know the answer. Well, my friends, I am brave enough to say that this is something that I have personally struggled with.

I can't help it! I have a lot to say, a lot of ideas, and a lot of opinions. However, I am learning that just because I think a lot of thoughts doesn't mean I need to continually share my opinion, especially when I become argumentative because I want to prove my point. So with much practice, I am learning to be a better listener. This means that I have to practice "active listening" while someone is speaking instead of thinking about what I am going to say back to that person immediately. Being an active listener takes a lot of self-discipline and practice.

With that said, if you also struggle in this area, instead of looking at it negatively, look at it as a gift that needs some minor adjusting. For instance, I might grow up to be a successful Attorney or Politician. Hey, you never know!

Keep in mind. It's okay to have opinions, thoughts, and ideas. Those are great things to have. Just be wise of when and how we share them and practice good listening skills. Being able to admit when we have areas that need attention is a quality that shows strength and good character. That is when we can grow and flourish. At least that's what my mom says!

I encourage you to strive to be an excellent listener!

LOVE

> 1 Corinthians 13:4-5
> "Love is patient, love is kind. It does not envy, it does not boast, it is not proud. It does not dishonor others, it is not self-seeking, it is not easily angered, it keeps no record of wrongs."

Agápē love is the highest form of love!

Agápē embraces a universal, unconditional love that transcends, that serves regardless of circumstances.

Wowzers, that was a mouth full. Ha! Grab the dictionary. In other words, LOVE is what is in the best interests of the other person, not yourself. Love is not an emotion or feeling. Love is a CHOICE! A choice to be patient, kind, understanding, respectful, and forgiving. If we all chose to Agápē love one another, our world would be a better place to live. Instead of finding faults in each other, we would seek understanding, common ground, and focus on the positive.

One of my favorite quotes is a wise word from Martin Luther King, Jr. "Darkness cannot drive out darkness; only light can do that. Hate cannot drive out hate; only love can do that."

Isn't that beautiful? I sure think so and agree wholeheartedly. Love is so powerful and would solve a lot of issues in our world if we all chose to walk in Agape love!

MIND YOUR BUSINESS

Hey, I found your nose.
It was in my business again.

Gossip, half-truths, passing judgment, and assumptions cause so many issues that arise in life. We would be wise to learn how to shut down conversations that are rooted in gossip, lies, and hurtful rumors of another person that only leads to pain.

My fourth-grade year was very hard for me because of this. Friendships that ended because of someone making up things that were not true and assumptions made about how I felt about a situation that was also not true. These made up lies quickly turned into an ugly web of hurt. And sadly at the end of all the unnecessary drama, no one wins. Now there is awkwardness where there used to be friendship. And for what?

Gossip spreads like wildfire, causing a path of
destruction that destroys everything in its way.

Friendships are meant to build up, not tear down.
No matter who it is, a person you know or don't know,
we should never believe or even listen to things that are
gossip. It's so sad how fast people will believe garbage
as truth. Keep in mind if that so-called friend is talking
bad about another person; ask yourself what are they
saying about you, behind your back?

If a conversation is not lifting someone up,
then shut that conversation down
and move on.

No

Have you ever heard the saying,
"Let your no be no, and your yes be yes?"

In life, there will be many times when someone will ask us for things, and our answer is "no" just as there will be times we will ask for things and people will tell us "no."

Saying no can be challenging. Most people want to make others happy and saying 'no' can seem like we are unkind. There are many different reasons why someone's answer could be no. But there are also times where we will want to say yes and just can't. Or you don't agree with their request at all, and that is okay. Bottom line is we should always respect their decision and move on.

I know that kids our age are usually scared to say no because we don't want to lose a friend or start a fight. But no one should ever feel pressured to do something they don't want to do. You should also never feel guilty because you said no to someone's request. Of course, we don't want to seem rude or hurt another's feelings, but we also have to protect ourselves and set good boundaries.

If you are afraid of losing a friendship because your answer to their request is no, you might want to re-evaluate that friendship. It is not healthy to worry always if someone will stop being your friend.

Friendships should be understanding, loving, kind, and respectful, always.

After giving something much thought if your answer is no, here are a few ways to say no in a friendly way.

- "No, thank you."
- "I wish I could help you out, but I can't."
- "That's awesome, but I'm unavailable."
- "I already have plans, maybe another time."
- "I don't agree with that, so I will have to pass."
- "Thank you for inviting me, but I can't make it."
- "This doesn't fit my schedule but maybe another time."

Another saying that we have all heard our parents say is, "If one of your friends jumped off of a bridge, would you?" sometimes the person you are saying no to is YOURSELF! You may be tempted to do something you know is wrong, but you have to tell yourself, "No!" we are all faced with decisions every day that require us to make choices. We might not think of it so literally, but we tell ourselves yes and no all the time. Will you partake in a lie? If a friend told you to steal something, would you? Would you cheat on your homework? Would you be mean to a classmate because your friend doesn't like that person?

Will you make the right decisions when given the opportunity? Especially when you want to take a cookie from the cookie jar, and your mom said, "no more cookies?!"

OPPORTUNITY

Definition: A set of circumstances that makes it possible to do something.

Do you think about your future?

I'm so excited to live in a time where there are so many choices, open doors, and paths ahead of me. Think about it! How do you imagine your life? Right now, we have our whole lives ahead of us. We are young; we can choose to be anything we want to be.

Life is a journey full of opportunities that can lead us down various paths.

When I grow up, I want to be: an actor, an artist, or maybe an inventor. I haven't made up my mind! There are so many choices!

Seriously, the possibilities are endless; firefighter, police officer, designer, doctor, architect, mechanic, librarian, business owner, teacher, lawyer, soldier, nurse, pastor, farmer, computer programmer, pilot... the list could go on and on, but what do you want to be when you grow up?

You know that list above, of all those cool careers? Well, every day, we have a chance or opportunity to work towards that goal. And we have a choice to either work hard every day or to work just a little. The word opportunity is a way of saying that you have the gift of a chance that could result in getting what you really want, but only if you are willing to work for it.

Seeking opportunities is a way of opening doors, but no one can carry you through the door. That's the hard part, and it's up to you to not just to follow your dreams but to hunt them down and achieve them. Seek, and you will find it. Knock, and the door will be opened to you. I heard this in church, and it always stuck in my mind. We can see our dreams, but until we see the opportunity to knock on the door, it will never be a reality.

I'm ready to start kicking some doors down!

"MOVE out of your comfort zone,
YOU can only GROW if you are willing to feel
awkward & uncomfortable when you try something new."
- Brian Tracy

\ \ \ \ \ \ \ \ \ \ \

P AIN

Definition: Physical or emotional suffering caused by injury, illness, or great unhappiness.

Pain is a feeling, physical or emotional. It can be in your heart or some part of your body. I would bet you if I asked someone, "Do you like pain?" They would say, "No!" But what would life be like if there was no pain? Now, you're probably thinking to yourself, "life would be perfect without pain!" The thought of having no pain at all is nice, but what if the pain was the driving force that caused you to do better?

Pain can be a way of learning, growing, and motivating us in life.

I believe as oxygen is to trees, pain is to humans! If trees didn't have oxygen they would die, which would be unfortunate for us humans because we need oxygen to breathe. Trees breathe in carbon dioxide, which is bad for us, and then breathe out life-giving oxygen. The same way we as people can live through our pain and breathe life into those around us.

My family loves to hike. We have been going on one particular hike every summer for the last five years, so since I was five years old. It's very challenging! A lot of trail goes straight up. Every time I do this hike, I think it will be easier since I do it every year, but somehow it beats my butt! I feel pain in my legs, hips, essentially everywhere! I get so tired. At times I hate it and want just to give up. If I focus only on the pain, I can't think of anything else, and I wonder, "why does my mom make me go on this hike every single year?" But then I change my focus from the pain to the goal of finishing. I put one foot in front of the other and keep on going. Before I know it, I'm at the top of the mountain embracing the beauty before me and eating lunch!

This type of physical pain, although temporary, could have stopped me from fulfilling my goal of getting to the top of the mountain. I could have given up and turned around, I could of let that pain overtake me and make me think that I wasn't physically fit enough to finish it. But I don't want to be that kind of person. I don't want to give up. I want to do my best and face my mountains in life and conquer them!

Another kind of pain is emotional. When I was in ice skating lessons, we were learning how to do cross-overs. If you are wondering what a cross-over is, in short, it's when you are skating in a circle, taking one foot and crossing it over your other foot. It's meant to teach you how to turn easily.

Now skating on ice is hard. It might come naturally to some, but for me, it's something that I have to work on, which is why I take classes. In my first class of learning cross-overs, I was struggling. A few of the kids who could do it easily would pass me and whisper, "come on just do it, it's so simple" "everyone else can do it, but you" "What's so hard about it?" This taunting would happen EVERY SINGLE TIME they passed me. It hurt, it was frustrating; I couldn't focus because these things only brought my spirit down. I didn't even know these kids. Why were they so mean and hurtful to me? I wanted to cry; I wanted to give up! But then I had a thought while they just kept on passing by me trying to discourage me. Instead of letting their hurtful words destroy me, I will make it motivate me. Several classes later and tons of practice I now do cross-overs.

Today I encourage you to never give up no matter how much pain you feel, physically or emotionally.

QUESTION

Definition:
1. To ask questions in order to get information.
2. To have suspicions or doubt about something.

We live in a world where information is at our fingertips and it's great. We walk around with computers in our pockets and bags. With iPhones, laptops, and iPads finding information on any given subject is just seconds away. I don't personally have a cell phone yet, but I have access to my parents, and one of my favorite things to do is look up song lyrics.

With so much information available to us, we are also bombarded with other's opinions and false reports. News articles, blogs, Facebook, Instagram, YouTube, funny memes the list goes on. Information is available every second of every day, and it spreads around social media like wildfire good and bad. We, humans, suck it up and believe it all as truth. If a celebrity thinks that way, I should. If a singer said it, it must be true. This is a trap! Without much consideration or source checking, we hit share and become a part of spreading false information.

I was watching a show one day called "Brain Games." The episode was an experiment on individuals and how they respond to questions in a group setting. The experiment showed that when asked questions, the majority of people chose the answer of their peers, which happened to be the wrong answer. The one person who decided to go out on his or her own was the one correct. Over and over again, this experiment showed this behavior. The point is just because someone or many people think something, that doesn't mean they're right. It is essential to ask important questions, gather accurate information, and form your own opinion based on facts.

Knowledge is power!

So how do we know if something is true or false? We do a simple fact check. It only takes a few extra steps to research something to verify and see if the information you are reading on social media is true, false, or merely someone's opinion. Another way is getting an adult, like a parent or a teacher to help you research. If you don't want to take the time to fact check then don't share it.

My parents tell me to question everything and to ask myself a few simple questions. I will share them with you:

1. Where is this information originating?
2. What is the purpose of this information?
3. Is this information fact or opinion?
4. Is this information causing division or helping?
5. How is this information serving our world and purpose?

Remember just because it's on the Internet doesn't mean its true!

R ELATIONSHIPS

Definition – The way in which people feel about and behave toward one another.

It is important to surround yourself with healthy relationships. Building a strong community of friendships is essential. I don't believe in having just one "best friend." I desire to be open to new friendships. When you place one person in your life with that title, you are putting that friendship over all your other friendships. Of course, you will have certain people that you mesh better with and do more things with but avoiding certain labels will create a more inviting spirit.

My mom has taught me that there are three main types of friendships.

1. Give / Give – This friendship is always giving and receiving. You invite them, and they invite you.

You encourage them, and they encourage you. Always serving one another.

2. Give / Take – This friendship one is giving more than the other. For example, Your friend is going through a rough situation and not 100%. You are the one continually encouraging, uplifting, and helping or visa versa.

3. Seasonal – This friendship was in your life for a season. Either to teach you something or for you to teach them something. Then you move on for whatever reason.

When we understand the cycle of friendships in our lives, it is easier not to take things so personally. When a seasonal friendship ends, it doesn't hurt so much cause you understand that there was a purpose to that person being in your life and now for whatever reason, that season has ended. Or when you feel that you are giving into a friendship more than you are receiving you can evaluate if that friend is just in a bad place and needs you or if it is an unhealthy relationship and you need to move on. The important thing to keep in mind is that none of these are bad.

I had a close friend in my 2nd and 3rd-grade years of school. We played together every day at recess. We got together on the weekends and had sleepovers and had a ton of fun together. 4th grade came; we were in different classes and made new friends. We slowly drifted apart, and she no longer wanted to be friends with me. It hurt, I missed her, and at the time I didn't understand but soon realized that we had both changed. We no longer had much in common. In life, we are all growing and changing constantly, and sometimes that means who makes a good fit as a friend may begin to change, too!

The important thing to remember is always to keep your circle open and ready to invite new friendships in. Look for things you have in common and do those activities together. One friend you might enjoy hiking with because you both love to exercise together and another friend you might like to dress up together as Chewbacca and Princess Leia and head to the theater every time a new Star Wars movie comes out and another friend you might want to have a book club with because you both love to read. You get the point; you can have several relationships that are diverse from one another that you get together with to do different things.

A healthy friendship:

- Enjoys being with you
- Encourages you to do your best.
- Listens to you.
- Tries to make you feel better when you're feeling down.
- Doesn't gossip about you or others.
- Is honest.
- Stands up for you and their other friends.
- Laughs with you, not at you.
- Makes time for you.
- Welcomes new friends into your circle.
- Is kind to you and other people.
- Admits when they are wrong and apologizes.

"WE often take for GRANTED the very things
that most DESERVE our gratitude."
- Cynthia Ozick

\ \ \ \ \ \ \ \ \ \

Stay in your lane

We are churchgoers, so we hear a lot of awesome catchphrases and this one by Pastor Robert Madu we like to repeat often in our home.

"Stay in your lane!"

What does this mean exactly? Well at the core it means NOT to have an opinion about something that you don't have first-hand experience with. For example, my big brother is a boxer. I in no way, shape, or form am going to try and give him advice about being a better boxer. I have no experience whatsoever in fighting techniques, proper form, punching, or blocking. All I know about boxing is how to cheer him on while he is in the ring fighting.

I hear about this topic a lot because my parents opened up their own business a few years ago. At their business, they often hear, "Hey, you know what you should do?" or "Hey, you need to buy this or that." However, most of these individuals don't own a business of their own; have no clue what it's like to build a business from the ground up let alone run one.

Did you know it's okay NOT to have an opinion about something? We live in a world that is full of opinions. People who share their thoughts on every subject as if they are experts on any given topic. Because every person's experiences and paths are different, there is no way we could know "the answer" to every problem or even have a valid opinion without knowing all the history, facts and various variables that go with every issue of life.

Let's practice understanding one another verses giving unwanted opinions. My parents encourage me to try and look at situations through another perspective and not just my own. It takes practice, but if we can create this habit, you will learn to bite your tongue, be more understanding and stay in your lane!

TEAMWORK

Definition: The combined action of a group of people, especially when effective and efficient.

As my fourth grade teacher, Mr. Estella would always say, "Teamwork makes the dream work! "

Teamwork is the key to success. When we build community and work together towards a common goal, we can accomplish way more than if we tried to do something on our own.

As I mentioned before, my dad and mom opened their own business a few years ago, and boy was it a lot of hard work, dedication, and time. I watched them for months, create, build, and work together to open up a business that was my dad's dream. From being covered in sawdust to now a thriving business where hundreds of people come weekly is such an amazing thing that I got to experience and be a part of.

69

They set a goal, made a plan, and worked together to achieve it!

As students, we can do the same thing. Whether it be working on school projects, playing sports on a team, volunteering in your community, participating in a play, playing an instrument in a band or raising money for a cause these are things that all require teamwork and coming together in unity to achieve a common goal.

Together we are better.
We were never created to do life alone!

U NIQUE

Definition: The only one of its kind; unlike anything else.

Look around. There is no one like you; You are the only one of YOU. You have your own unique personality, style, talents, and desires that are uniquely you. Right now, you may not know "all the things" and have everything figured out, and that is okay. Life is a journey, and we are all on an adventure discovering new things about ourselves every day. In life, we are continually learning, growing, and changing and will be for the rest of our lives.

How amazing is it that we come from different families, cultures, and backgrounds? All these things help shape our uniqueness and who we are. When people come together from different cultures, we learn and teach one another, and that is truly a beautiful thing. Being different is a great thing. We ALL have something to contribute. Imagine if we were all the same, liked the same things, looked the same, acted the same. The world would be so dull. Diversity is one of the best blessings God could have ever given us. So don't try and be like anyone else. Our differences are what makes this world such a fantastic place.

Do you and BE YOU!

You have a purpose and a destiny. I believe we all have different paths that we need to take in life. And we all have something to contribute to the world to help make it a better place. There are people you will meet, that I will never meet. There are people that you are supposed to be friends with that I will never be a friend to. There are people that you are supposed to help that I will never help. Not because I don't want to but because I will never cross paths with them and you will. Everyone has a different purpose to fulfill, but there is one universal mission that we are all responsible for doing, and that is to walk in love.

To walk in love you can't play the compare game. Comparing yourself to others is a trap that will lead you down a road of feeling awful about yourself. The bottom line, comparing yourself to others is not healthy. We are all different sizes, shapes, and beautiful shades of color. So instead of comparing and judging build people up, embrace all those unique qualities and celebrate our differences!

We all have a unique beauty inside of us.

Volunteer

Volunteer - a person who does something, for other people or for an organization, willingly and without being forced or paid to do it.

Live to Give, Love to Give

I have grown up hearing this quote. In our home, we believe in helping others. Volunteering and serving in any way that we can. Whenever I volunteer my time, it makes me feel so good inside. When you share your time, giving to others, it shows that you care, desire to help and want to be a part of the solution.

There is so much going on all around us. Everyone's schedules are full of work, school, activities, family functions, sports, and life; it can be easy to forget that there are people all around us that need help. Some people are hungry, don't have a place to live, need clothes, shoes… help! AND they also need LOVE, a kind smile, a hug, and a nice gesture.

Volunteering helps our community and our world.

There are so many ways you can get involved and start serving. One of the places I love to volunteer at is my church. Every year we do a backpack drive where hundreds of kids come and get a free backpack full of school supplies. We also do a huge Thanksgiving drive where we pass out thousands of Thanksgiving dinners to families who cant afford it. Going to a local church is a great place to go to find opportunities to volunteer. Also, there are tons of local organizations, community centers, shelters, charities, and non-profit businesses that love people to come and volunteer their time as well.

Did you know that you could go to nursing homes and spend time with elderly people? Do you play a musical instrument? Do you like to do crafts, plant flowers, or read out loud? Some elderly people don't have family nearby and would love some company.

What about animals? Did you know you could volunteer at a local farm or zoo? My older sister volunteered at a goat rescue ranch for two years and loved it. I loved it too because when we would drop her off, I used to be able to go and pet all the goats.

What if you organized a neighborhood or local park garbage pickup? There seems to be more and more garbage being tossed out car windows and thrown on the sides of our roads. I walk to school and the whole way to school, I see tons of garbage all on the sidewalk and grass. Sometimes we have filled a full bag of waste just walking to and from school. Do you litter? I sure hope not!

Have you ever heard of the saying, "it is better to give than to receive?" When I Volunteer, I can feel this quote. I get so much satisfaction in helping others. Knowing that I did something to help put a smile on a person's face is very rewarding. It's like a victory that you have accomplished in triumph. Let's all do our part in making our world a better place to live in. I believe it's done by showing compassion, serving and loving others.

Have I inspired you to start Volunteering? I sure hope so! I urge you to find a place that you can volunteer sometimes. I promise you will feel so good inside knowing you contributed and care about our society and the people who live in it.

I found this cool list of ways you can volunteer your time on a website called PrepScholar. I'm listing a few,

but if you want to see more options go to:
https://blog.prepscholar.com/129-examples-of-community-service-projects

- Donate your old clothes,
- Volunteer at a soup kitchen,
- Donate non-perishable food to a food bank,
- Donate blankets to a homeless shelter,
- Host a Thanksgiving dinner for people who can't afford their own,
- Make "care kits" with shampoo, toothbrushes, combs, etc. to donate to homeless shelters,
- Donate art supplies to kids in a homeless shelter,
- Help organize and sort donations at a homeless shelter,
- Babysit children while their parents look for jobs,
- Build flower boxes for Habitat for Humanity houses,
- Organize a winter clothes drive to collect coats, hats, scarves, and gloves to be donated,
- Make first aid kits for homeless shelters,
- Take care of cats and dogs at an animal shelter,
- Clean up a local park,
- Start a butterfly garden in your community,
- Foster animals that shelters don't have space for,
- Build and set up a birdhouse,
- Plant native flowers or plants along highways,

- Read to residents at a nursing home,
- Mow an elderly neighbor's lawn,
- Make birthday cards for the elderly,
- Donate and decorate a Christmas tree at a nursing home,
- Ask residents of a retirement home to tell you about their lives,
- Perform a concert or play at a senior center,
- Help elderly neighbors clean their homes and organize their belongings,
- Rake leaves, shovel snow, or wash windows for a senior citizen.

"Work for a cause, not for applause.
Live life to express, not to impress."
- Grace Lichtenstein

\ \ \ \ \ \ \ \ \ \

WORK FOR A CAUSE

I read this quote by Grace Lichtenstein and instantly loved it, "Work for a cause, not for applause. Live life to express, not to impress."

"Work for a cause."

Now you are probably thinking "Meadow I'm in elementary school or junior high school. I'm not thinking about a job!" Ha, and either am I. However, what I take from this quote is all about MOTIVE. The motives behind "why" we do something can completely change the whole meaning behind what we are doing. For example, If I help a person just to be recognized but didn't mean it from the heart, I have now tainted what should have been something good. My intentions were all about recognition instead of just being a good friend.

Do everything from a spirit of goodness, not from a place of selfishness.

When we work hard at school; help a classmate, be a good friend, get our homework done on time, be there for our teammates, do all our chores without our parents having to remind us, we are contributing, doing our part and working for a cause and not for applause!

"Live life to express, not to impress."

How are you expressing your true self?; What do you like? What interests do you have? What are your passions? Are you genuinely being authentic in how you express yourself? Or are you just putting on a show and living life to impress?

Be true to yourself; be real, be authentic!

 X MARKS THE SPOT

> "Think LEFT and think RIGHT
> and think LOW and think HIGH oh
> the things you can think up if only you try"
>
> - Dr. Suess

X marks the spot is all about goals!

I like to envision a treasure map. The map shows you how to get to your treasure. The treasure (the big red X on the map) is your goal, and all those tiny lines that lead up to your wealth are the different steps you need to take to get to your treasure (your goal).

In our house, we set goals all the time. Goals should be a regular part of your life. Having goals keeps you moving forward. Keeping you being productive, motivated, and giving you something to always look forward to. There are so many areas in life to set goals. Here are a few to think about:

- Fitness goals,
- Healthy eating goals,
- Educational goals,
- Book goals,
- Hiking goals,
- Writing goals,
- Traveling goals,
- Business goals (you are never too young.)

The list could go on and on. There are endless amounts of goals that you can come up with. You can create small goals or big goals. For example, a fitness goal could be as little as doing 20 squats a day or as big as running 3 miles 3 times a week. Healthy eating goals could be as small as eating one banana every morning or as big as drinking a certain amount of glasses of water every day. Book goals could be as little as reading one book for pleasure a year or as big as three books per month. There are no rules to setting goals. It's personal and what you feel will help you to move forward. Your goals will look different than mine, and that is okay. I love to read and set book goals, but you might like sports and set goals that are more physical.

Last year I set a goal for myself in January that I wanted to be one of the few kids that are a part of the 100+ points Accelerated Reader program at my school. Even though the average AR goal is around 30 for my age at the time, I love reading and wanted to challenge myself. And I am proud to say that I accomplished that goal by the end of the school year and proudly collected my certificate. It took a lot of discipline and dedication. I had a book in my hand continually, but I had my goal in mind and was determined to accomplish it.

You might be wondering how to come up with a goal. All you need to do is see what you want in the future and go after it. What are your goals? What is something you want to achieve? I would encourage you to search your heart, find things that interest you, and set some goals.

Then map out the steps that will help you get to your treasure.

Yesterday

"Yesterday is history, tomorrow is a mystery, But today is a gift. That's why we call it the present." - A.A. Milne

I recently went to the movies and saw a movie called, Overcomer with my mom. It was about a girl named Hanna who never met her father and believed he had died. She later discovers that her dad was alive but in poor health in the hospital. He had made a lot of mistakes in his past, but she chose to forgive him. Instead of holding onto yesterday and what happened, she decided to look to the future. It was such an inspiring movie to watch about overcoming in many ways.

Sometimes it can be hard to let go of the past. Remembering painful moments that continually replay in your mind can cause you so much heartache. It's important to not focus on the pain of yesterday but on the hope of tomorrow.

We all make mistakes in life. The cool thing is that we all have the power to change. Every day is a new opportunity to start over. No matter how small or how big of a mistake you make. Don't beat yourself up about it. Apologize when you need to, learn from it, change the behavior, and forgive yourself!

Cue Disney's Frozen song "Let it Go"

Zip It

"Words are powerful, and they have consequences"
- Karen Ehman

Have you ever said something to someone and instantly regret it? I know I sure have. Sometimes it sounds a whole lot better in your head than when it comes out. Even when your intention wasn't to be mean, sometimes we say stupid things.

Like I have stated before, I can sometimes seem argumentative while trying to prove a point. I have to zip it and practice being an "active listener" instead of thinking about what I will say next to defend my point. We all have things we struggle with, and this is one of mine.

Our words are so powerful. They can build a person up, or they can tear a person down. I personally never want to hurt anyone. Being a person that is slow to speak and quick to listen with understanding is who I strive to be.

We don't need to say everything that comes into our minds. I encourage you to be intentional with the words you speak. It is better to say nothing at all than to say something unkind.

In what ways do you think you may be able to respond differently to receive a peaceful reaction? Not to argue with someone or prove a point, but to truly understand. In many ways zipping it is just out of mere consideration for those around you and complete self-awareness to be the best you, you can be.

Keys to Zipping It:
-Truly listen to the other person.
-Pause and self evaluate.
-Put other's feelings into account before responding.
-Reply with kindness.
-Respond in a way you hope to receive.

It's okay to AGREE to DISAGREE.

With these steps, communication within friendships, family, and classmates should help you to choose your words wisely and contribute to having healthy respectful relationships.

Thank you so much for reading my book!

Meadow Faith

```
L E G G D S U P B E V A R B C
R C L N E L R J S M E K M T O
N E O O T A H V O V E F G O U
H I V R I O Y V I U B O L D R
F P E T C G Q T Q K R R D Y A
L R X S X L I I I Y D G T I G
A E I G E S N N O O Y I Q K E
U T L E O U D Y M J N V C P O
G S W P N N E O B U P E L E U
H A Z L E D D J T K O N K A S
T M Y S Q S S R E Z X E U C K
E I S K I K O H T F V S C E D
R Q R W P P F U I K I S T C T
O A G A P E T L I P K L S F C
D H K O C U E B E L I E V E I
```

AGAPE	OPPORTUNITY
BELIEVE	PEACE
BOLD	POSITIVE
BRAVE	STRONG
COURAGEOUS	UNIQUE
EXCITED	WISDOM
FORGIVENESS	
FRIENDSHIP	
GOALS	
JOY	
KINDNESS	
LAUGHTER	
LIFE	
LOVE	
MASTERPIECE	

Word Scramble

Unscramble the words.

1. hnipiefdrs _____
2. osgnrt _____
3. phlefou _____
4. etrcieepmas _____
5. itisevpo _____
6. yesvtdrii _____
7. dolb _____
8. ossipaomnc _____
9. eusrucagoo _____
10. ualrhtge _____
11. eabvr _____
12. nekndssi _____
13. ienuuq _____

14. gsfioerensv _____
15. losag _____
16. tonrioppuyt _____
17. miwsdo _____
18. aegap _____
19. txceedi _____
20. emdwao _____
21. nte _____
22. leov _____
23. nhgoetesrtse _____
24. ldsseeb _____
25. fthai _____

Word Box

masterpiece	agape	compassion	love
courageous	positive	diversity	goals
kindness	bold	brave	excited
blessed	meadow	forgiveness	laughter
togetherness	strong	hopeful	friendship
ten	unique	opportunity	wisdom
faith			

Shop

Check out
www.meadowfaith.com

Follow on Instagram
itsmeadowfaith

Strong
BOLD
Courageous
www.meadowfaith.com

Meadow
Faith

Free
Bookmark
Cutout

Made in the USA
Middletown, DE
28 September 2019